Am I Fit and Healthy?

LEARNING ABOUT DIET AND EXERCISE

WAYLAND

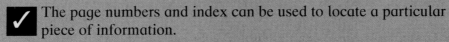

All Wayland books encourage children to read and help them improve their literacy.

✓ The page numbers and index can be used to locate a particular piece of information.

✓ The glossary reinforces alphabetic knowledge and extends vocabulary.

✓ The books to read section suggests other books dealing with the same subject.

First published in 1998 by
Wayland Publishers Ltd

This edition published in 2007 by Wayland,
an imprint of Hachette Children's Books

© Copyright 1998 Wayland
All rights reserved

Hachette Children's Books
338 Euston Road London, NW1 3BH

British Library Cataloguing in Publication Data
Llewellyn, Claire
Am I Fit and Healthy? : learning about diet and exercise. (Me and my body)
1.Diet – Juvenile literature 2. Nutrition – Juvenile literature 3. Exercise – Juvenile literature
I. Title II. Gordon, Mike 1948 – 613.2

ISBN 978 0 7502 5273 7

Printed and bound in China

ME AND MY BODY series:
Am I Fit and Healthy?
  LEARNING ABOUT DIET AND EXERCISE

Nice or Nasty?
  LEARNING ABOUT DRUGS AND YOUR HEALTH

Where Did I Come From?
A FIRST LOOK AT SEX EDUCATION

Why Wash?
LEARNING ABOUT PERSONAL HYGIENE

Am I Fit and Healthy?

LEARNING ABOUT DIET AND EXERCISE

Written by Claire Llewellyn
and
illustrated by Mike Gordon

Everyone needs to eat food.

You need to eat bags
and bags of it every
week.

Food gives you energy.

It helps you grow and be fit and healthy.

metres

When you were born, you
only ate one food – milk,
which made you grow ...

Hic!

6

And ... grow! Quite soon, you ate lots of other foods, too. They helped you grow even more.

As you grew older, you wanted some foods more than others. Sometimes you wanted biscuits instead of your meal.

8

But you're old enough to eat
sensibly now ...

... Aren't you?

Eating sensibly means eating all sorts of foods.

Every food helps your body in a different kind of way.

Some foods help to build your body.

Some foods give you energy.

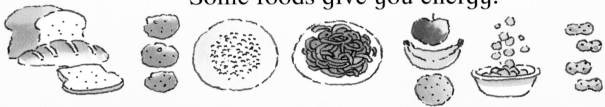

Other foods keep your body working properly.

These foods help you to store up energy.

Don't forget water is good for you, too.

Make sure your body gets everything it needs by eating many different kinds of food.

This is called a healthy diet.

But watch out!

You can eat too much of some
kinds of food ...

Too many sweet and
fatty foods will ...

rot your teeth ...

give you spots ...

help you to put on weight ...

and make you ill when
you're older.

We all need to eat the right amount
of food for our own body.

Growing children usually eat
more than older people.

Somebody big usually needs
more to eat than someone
small.

Eating more than you need makes your body fat, especially if you eat the wrong kinds of food.

Different people choose and enjoy different kinds of food.

But sometimes they have a special reason for saying no.

Whatever you like or don't like to eat, try to eat a healthy diet.

It will help you to:

... grow

... fight off germs and sicknesses

... work, think and understand

... be active and full of beans.

Keeping active makes your muscles bigger and your bones stronger.

It helps your lungs to
work better, too, and
gives you lots of puff.

When you're active, you often feel full of life.

When you're not active, you feel rather flat.

Different people keep active in many different ways.

Why not do activities you enjoy with a parent or friend?

It'll make you all feel better.

Your body is precious. Just look at what it can do. Your body can...

... think

... feel

... and do.

You *own* your body and you have to look after it.

Are you giving it the food and exercise it deserves?

So are you fit and healthy?

TOPIC WEB

Maths
Find out how much your family spends on food each week. Find out how much people of different ages eat by asking them all the same set of questions about their meals.

Design and Technology
Look at different games and activities and consider how safe they are, e.g. cycling, skipping. What are the risks involved in each one, and how can the activity be made safer?

History
Ask grandparents about the sports and games they played as children. Find out what their favourite foods were and whether they are still popular or available today.

Science
Think of different ways of classifying and grouping different foods that you eat, e.g. very good for you, good for you, good in small amounts, etc.

Geography
Find out about the eating and exercise habits of children in another locality currently being studied, and compare them with those of your class.

Am I Fit and Healthy?

R.E.
Find out about different religious customs relating to food from people in the school who practise them. Invite visitors from different faiths into school to talk about food.

Language
Write and illustrate a food diary, showing what you ate over a weekend. Find poems about food. Decide which one you like the best and write your own food poem.

Art and Craft
Make a collage of images of children enjoying sports and games, designed to encourage others to do more exercise.

Music
Find as many songs about food as possible. In a group, choose a song that lends itself to sound effects, and work out an accompaniment using different musical instruments.

P.E./Dance/Drama
Develop a simple playground game using a ball and involving running, jumping, skipping or other vigorous activity, so that the players will get plenty of exercise in break time.

GLOSSARY

active Doing things that use up energy.

diabetic A person whose body cannot make energy from sugars.

energy The power that comes from your body that makes you active.

germs Tiny forms of animal or plant life – some which cause illnesses.

lungs The parts of your chest that are used for breathing.

muscles Fleshy parts of the body which help you to move.

BOOKS TO READ

Healthy Eating by A series of books for young readers that looks at ways of keeping healthy.

Exercise and your Health by Jillian Powell (Health Matters series, Wayland, 2002)

For slightly older readers. Looks at benefits of exercise on your body and how to make exercise fun.

Food and Your Health by Jillian Powell (Health Matters series, Wayland, 2002)

For slightly older readers. Looks at the different types of foods available and how they help to keep your body healthy.

INDEX

active 21, 22, 24, 25, 26

activities 26

body 10, 11, 12, 16, 17, 28, 29

bones 22

eating 9, 10, 12, 13, 17

energy 5, 11

exercise 29

fat 14, 17

food 4, 5, 6, 7, 8, 10, 11, 12, 13, 16, 17, 18, 29

growth 5, 6, 7, 8, 16, 21

lungs 23

milk 6

muscles 22

sickness 15, 21

spots 15

sweets 14

teeth 14

weight 15